THE LIVING GOSPEL

Daily Devotions for Advent 2020

110669527

THE LIVING GOSPEL

Daily Devotions for Advent 2020

Charles Paolino

AVE MARIA PRESS AVE Notre Dame, Indiana

Founded in 1865, Ave Maria Press is a ministry of the United States Province of Holy Cross.

www.avemariapress.com

Paperback: ISBN-13 978-1-59471-993-6

E-book: ISBN-13 978-1-59471-994-3

Cover image "Approaching Bethlehem" © 2012 by Jeni Butler, artworkbyjeni.wiz.com/art.

Cover and text design by John R. Carson.

Printed and bound in the United States of America.

INTRODUCTION

In the summer of 2016, Pope Francis had an appointment with his dentist, whose office is within the boundaries of the Vatican State, but—Francis being Francis—he made a detour on the way back.

When the pope was done at the dentist, he told the security officer who was driving him to go to the office of the Pontifical Commission for Latin America, which was nearby but in the city of Rome, outside the confines of the Vatican.

The security officer told Francis that this would be complicated because no one had been informed that Francis would be leaving the Vatican, and there was a procedure in place to prepare for a papal visit to the office.

Francis told him, in effect, "I am the pope. Don't worry about it."

In a few minutes, Francis was ringing the doorbell at the commission's office, and when a stunned employee opened the door, the pope said, "Good morning. May I come in?"

I was reminded of this incident as I read the gospel passage for Mass on the First Sunday of Advent. Both Francis's visit and the gospel passage feature the abrupt appearance of an authority figure, but there's a big difference between the tone of the gospel reading and the tone of the visit from Pope Francis.

The parable from Mark's gospel sounds ominous, as it warns servants that the master might burst in suddenly and catch the servants off guard. Jesus doesn't say what the master would do if he found his servants sleeping, but the implication is that it wouldn't be good. In the case of Pope Francis's surprise visit, there was none of that menacing atmosphere. The staff at the office

Francis visited was holding a meeting about the pope's upcoming trip to South America and, after the initial shock wore off, they were delighted to see him and even more delighted that he stayed for coffee.

Although these two scenes are so different in mood, they really are two sides of the same coin. The parable reminds us that we each have moral responsibilities that are spelled out in the Commandments and in the teaching of Jesus and his Church. These responsibilities include respecting and worshiping God, obeying just laws, treating other people with dignity and justice, doing everything we can to care for people who are in material or spiritual need, and sustaining and protecting the environment. The parable tells us that we can't attend to these responsibilities only when it suits us, but that we must be conscious of them every hour of every day and allow them to guide all of our decisions and actions.

That's why Jesus says, "Be watchful. Be alert." Because to be a true disciple of his is to be his disciple in everything we do, and we will in some way be measured by how well we live up to this calling. It helps to know that Jesus made these remarks at the end of a disturbing lesson: His apostles had pointed out to him the size and magnificence of the Temple in Jerusalem, and Jesus had responded by pointedly reminding them that nothing is permanent—not this building and not their own lives. There will be an end, so, "Be watchful. Be alert."

But the same Jesus who sobered up his apostles with this blunt message also taught in his preaching, and by his own example, that the fact that God has given us standards to live by does not mean that God is hiding in the shrubbery so that he can pounce on us when we go off the rails. I'm sorry to say that many people have been left with that impression by their religious education.

No, the central teaching of both the Jewish and Christian faiths is that God's desire is not to condemn us, but rather to save us. That's why Jesus, as his critics loved to point out, ate with sinners and prostitutes.

This has been a constant theme of Pope Francis, who sets a high standard of moral responsibility, but who also conspicuously goes out of his way to embrace people regardless of their religious faith or their station in life. He eschews formality and seeks to connect with people in their everyday situations.

The title of one of Francis's most important documents is *Evangelii Gaudium (The Joy of the Gospel)*, and he has again and again stressed the idea that the Church can thrive and grow not with discouragement and condemnation, but only with joy. That joy comes from our faith that God loves us regardless of our mistakes—that he loves us for the good that we do and for the persistence with which we repent and rebound when we have failed.

It's in that spirit that Francis brushes aside security and protocol, asks his own employee, "May I come in?" and then stays for coffee. He doesn't want the pope or the Church itself, which represents God on earth, to appear cold or remote, but rather eager to accompany all people on their human journey.

These are appropriate thoughts as we begin this Advent season in which we anticipate two things—our celebration of the birth of Jesus and the Second Coming of Jesus at the end of time. This is not a penitential season, as Lent is, but it is a season for contemplation of our relationship with God and with each other, a season to begin again, surely pleasing a God who abhors death and loves new beginnings.

SUNDAY, NOVEMBER 29
FIRST WEEK OF ADVENT

BEGIN

Let your heart prepare him room.

PRAY

> Would that you might meet us doing right, that we
> were mindful of you in our ways!
>
> ~*Isaiah 64:4a*

LISTEN

Read Mark 13: 33–37.

> Jesus said to his disciples: "Be watchful! Be alert! You
> do not know when the time will come."
>
> ~*Mark 13:33*

Returning God's Love

The head of a company I once worked for vacationed for
several weeks each year. His office door was left open,
and the lights were on every day of his absence. He was
in many ways a benign employer, but—whatever he
intended—the open door and the glowing lights implied
that employees should be on their toes because the boss
might return at any minute.

Some employees may have acted responsibly for
that reason, and some may have done so to protect their
livelihoods. Most would have been on their toes whether
the boss was on the premises or not—because they took
pride in their work or because they thought it was the
right thing to do.

Now consider today's gospel passage. Although Jesus' remarks are often interpreted to mean that folks should avoid sin because they could die at any time and face God while in an embarrassing condition, we can interpret his message in a more constructive way, and especially during the season of Advent. During Advent, we anticipate our celebration of the birth of Jesus, the event in which God appeared in history in the form of a human being. God did not appear in this way to frighten humanity into submission. Rather, through this act of unconditional love, God provided us with a way to intimacy with the Divine, and that way was Jesus' Gospel of love, charity, and justice, and the example of his life of compassion and humility.

Advent reminds us to measure the large and small decisions that we make every day by the standard of his teaching and his example. Refreshed by this season, we can continue striving for that ideal, not because we're afraid to be caught off guard, but because we want to return the love that God gave us in Jesus.

ACT

This evening, I will take a few moments to reflect on how my decisions and actions today reflected what Jesus taught.

PRAY

Lord Jesus Christ, with the help of the Holy Spirit, may I reflect your teaching and your example in every detail of my everyday life and especially in those actions that affect the lives of others. Amen.

BEGIN

Let your heart prepare him room.

PRAY

> Thus faith comes from what is heard, and what is heard comes through the word of Christ. But I ask, did they not hear? Certainly they did; for "Their voice has gone forth to all the earth, and their words to the ends of the world."

> ~*Romans 10:17–18a*

LISTEN

> *Read Matthew 4:18–22.*

> Jesus said to them, "Come after me, and I will make you fishers of men." At once they left their nets and followed him.

> ~*Matthew 4:19–20*

Start Spreading the News

A parishioner came to the sacristy after Mass one Sunday morning and asked me if I had a copy of an earlier homily. He said that I had preached it about six months before, and that the homily concerned a scripture passage he found difficult. He wanted to read again what I had said about it.

I searched my computer and found the homily, which I had actually preached about two-and-a-half years before, and the next time I saw the man I gave him a copy. When I handed it to him, he looked me in the eye and said, "You think we don't listen, don't you?" The incident reminded me that we preachers should be acutely aware that people *do* listen to what we say.

In fact, all Catholics should take this question to heart when we interact with Catholics and non-Catholics alike. All Catholics are commissioned by virtue of our baptism to carry on the ministry of St. Andrew the apostle, whose feast we celebrate today. The mission is to carry with us the Gospel of Jesus Christ wherever we go.

One tradition has it that St. Andrew preached the Gospel all around the Black Sea; another holds that he preached in Scotland. We don't have to travel that far to spread the Good News, and Advent provides us with a special opportunity to do so wherever we go with whomever we meet.

People will listen to us when we greet them during this season. Let them hear in the joy and warmth of our greeting that what we are preparing to celebrate is not the annual retail bonanza but the birth of Jesus, the one whose message of peace and love can still transform the world.

ACT

I will let others know as I greet them today that I am eager to celebrate the birth of my Savior.

PRAY

Dear Jesus, may my faith in you and my devotion to the Gospel guide everything that I say, and may nothing I say deny that you are Lord of my life. Amen.

Tuesday, December 1
First Week of Advent

BEGIN

Let your heart prepare him room.

PRAY

> There shall be no harm or ruin on all my holy mountain; for the earth shall be filled with knowledge of the LORD, as water covers the sea.
>
> *~Isaiah 11:9*

LISTEN

Read Luke 10:21–24.

> Jesus rejoiced in the Holy Spirit and said "I give you praise, Father, Lord of heaven and earth, for although you have hidden these things from the wise and the learned you have revealed them to the childlike."
>
> *~Luke 10:21*

First Things First

My grandson, age four, and granddaughter, age two, were discussing the use of a toy—a dialogue in which the word "mine" played a frequent and critical part. Their mother told the little girl to let her brother have his turn, to which he added, "Yes. That's called 'sharing'!"

We're often surprised when a young child makes a remark like that, but sometimes kids, whose lives are relatively simple, see more clearly than adults whose minds are cluttered with schemes and desires.

For centuries, scholars have studied the teachings of Jesus and worked to explain them further. Most of us don't have the time or the academic background to delve into the works of those philosophers and theologians, nor do we need to. After all, Jesus didn't teach out of textbooks; he talked to people in language they could understand and illustrated his teaching with stories drawn from the culture of that place and time.

In today's gospel passage, Jesus addresses a group of disciples who have returned from a successful missionary journey during which, we can imagine, they spread his teaching much as he had done. Jesus' comment to those disciples that what the Father had hidden "from the wise and learned" he had revealed "to the childlike" didn't mean that scholarship is useless or that faith-filled people are naïve.

Rather, it means that even before we study divine mysteries, we should commit ourselves completely to Jesus, the Son of God, making him the center of our lives. It means that we should make every other pursuit secondary to our most important pursuit—the one Jesus expressed as "the greatest commandment"—a daily life motivated by love of God and love of each other. And that's clear enough for a child to understand.

ACT

I will intentionally do a small act of patience, kindness, and generosity today, and thank God for making clear to me Jesus' commandment of love.

PRAY

Lord Jesus, help me to recognize each opportunity to live your commandment to love God and my fellow human beings unconditionally. May I always be attentive to the needs of others and help, comfort, or encourage them as though I were doing it for you. Amen.

WEDNESDAY, DECEMBER 2
FIRST WEEK OF ADVENT

BEGIN

Let your heart prepare him room.

PRAY

> On this mountain the LORD of hosts will provide for
> all peoples. . . . The Lord GOD will wipe away the
> tears from all faces.
>
> ~Isaiah 25:6a, 8a

LISTEN

Read Matthew 15:29–37.

> Then Jesus took the seven loaves and the fish, gave
> thanks, broke the loaves, and gave them to the disci-
> ples, who in turn gave them to the crowds. They all
> ate and were satisfied.
>
> ~Matthew 15: 36–37a

Feed the Hungry

Many Americans disdain Hebert Hoover, the thirty-first
President of the United States, for failing to deal with the
developing Great Depression of the 1930s. But others
lionize him for preventing the starvation of millions of
people—more than once.

Before his presidency, Hoover established a commission that arranged for millions of tons of food to be dis-
tributed to the people of Belgium after Germany invaded
the country in 1914 and refused to feed the people.
When the United States entered World War I, President
Woodrow Wilson appointed Hoover to manage food

production in the United States and provide supplies to the Allied Powers. Hoover's organization shipped twenty-five million tons of food to the Allies, saving them from collapse due to shortages in Europe.

After the war, with some four hundred million people in Europe facing starvation, Hoover was put in charge of feeding them, including the defeated Germans. During a famine that killed six million people in Russia shortly after the war, Hoover intervened to save millions more, answering critics who feared the Bolsheviks by saying, "Twenty million people are starving. Whatever their politics, they shall be fed!"

Hoover may not have been the only person who could have achieved those things, but for most people, the conditions he confronted would have seemed overwhelming, just as feeding the crowd seemed impossible to the apostles in the scene in Matthew's gospel. The message of this story is not that Jesus will perform miracles to feed the hungry, but that ordinary people can do more than they imagine to alleviate hunger and other forms of human suffering. One antidote to the consumerism that plagues Advent would be to bring food and water to a soup kitchen or food bank—not feeding millions, but feeding many who might go hungry if we choose to use our resources for a less compassionate purpose.

ACT

Today, I will eat a simple dinner at home and donate the money I could have spent dining out to a food bank.

PRAY

Dear Lord Jesus, through the influence of the Holy Spirit, give me an open heart to nourish others with food, clothing, my attention, and my prayers. As your disciples fed the crowd with the bread and fish that you gave them, may I share my gifts, in your name, with those in need. Amen.

Thursday, December 3
First Week of Advent

BEGIN

Let your heart prepare him room.

PRAY

> For the Lord is an eternal Rock. He humbles those in
> high places, and the lofty city he brings down.
>
> ~*Isaiah 26:4–5*

LISTEN

Read Luke 10:21–24.

> Jesus said to his disciples: "Not everyone who says to
> me, 'Lord, Lord,' will enter the Kingdom of heaven,
> but only the one who does the will of my Father in
> heaven."
>
> ~*Luke 10:23–24*

Open Your Heart

St. Francis Xavier, one of the founders of the Jesuit order,
was an eager missionary. In the sixteenth century, when
travel was difficult and dangerous, he joyfully carried the
Gospel to such far-flung places as Mozambique, Kenya,
India, and Japan. It was unusual for Europeans of that
era to wander so far from home, and Francis—a Basque
whose memorial we celebrate today—had to evolve in
his appreciation of the cultures that he encountered.

Although he remained single-minded in his deter-
mination to attract people to the Catholic faith, he himself was gradually transformed as he became more
comfortable among people of different origins. In fact,

he succeeded in his missions in part due to his ability to establish relationships with people of all sorts. He learned to speak other languages, and he wore apparel native to the cultures of the people he visited.

Francis himself had to undergo a conversion in which he learned that the different customs and beliefs of the people he encountered were not obstacles to his mission but rather opportunities to celebrate the variety of God's handiwork, and that God is present in all societies. In our contemporary society, and even in our Church, diversity can be a hot-button issue. There is a persistent tendency among many people to demean or fear cultures other than their own. But beginning with the visit of the Magi, the gospels tell us that the invitation to life in Christ is universal and unconditional. It is blind to culture, race, and nationality—in other words, catholic!

We are called in baptism to play a role in extending that invitation, to evangelize the world of our everyday lives. That means being respectful and welcoming to whomever we encounter—other Christians, yes, but Hindus, Muslims, and Buddhists as well, so that all can see in us the open arms and heart of Christ.

ACT

Today, I will be mindful of people in my parish and my community who may not share my background, and I will intentionally greet them in ways that make them feel welcome.

PRAY

Creator God, you make all things and disdain nothing that you have made. May I welcome people of all backgrounds, for, like me, they are your children. Amen.

Friday, December 4
First Week of Advent

BEGIN

Let your heart prepare him room.

PRAY

> On that day, the deaf shall hear the words of a book;
> and out of gloom and darkness, the eyes of the blind
> shall see.

> *~Isaiah 29:18*

LISTEN

Read Matthew 9:27–31.

> When he entered the house, the blind men
> approached him and Jesus said to them, "Do you
> believe that I can do this?" "Yes, Lord," they said to
> him. Then he touched their eyes and said, "Let it be
> done for you according to your faith." And their eyes
> were opened.

> *~Matthew 9:28–30a*

Put Your Faith in Him

A few years ago, my eye doctor told me that I was a
candidate for cataract surgery in both eyes. When the
doctor told me this, I immediately thought of my mater-
nal grandfather, who had cataract surgery in the early
1950s. He stayed with us while he convalesced—flat on
his back in a darkened room with sandbags on either
side to discourage him from moving his head.

But by the time I needed surgery, my ophthalmol-
ogist told me that the procedure on each eye would

take about twenty minutes and that when it was over, I would get up and walk away. This news was not reassuring to some of the folks I was working with at the time. They would shudder whenever the subject came up, and one woman kept asking me, "Ewwww, how can you let them operate on your *eyes*?" I told them that I didn't give it a second thought, because my surgeon was a pioneer in the particular procedure I would undergo; I had faith in him.

Faith is what today's gospel passage is all about. Two blind men pursue Jesus, because they have faith that he can heal them—and, I dare say, that he *would* heal them.

There are many stories like this one in the gospels, but the authors didn't record them to encourage us to call on Jesus to heal our physical ills. As remarkable as it is to cure someone's blindness, it doesn't compare to the healing that Jesus offers—freedom from the consequences of sin and death and, instead, life forever in the presence of God.

The healing that Jesus offers opens our eyes to the futility of earthly attachments and invites us to put our faith only in him, and to imitate his example of compassion, generosity, and forgiveness.

ACT

Today, I will schedule a time to receive the Sacrament of Reconciliation during this Advent season with faith in God's compassion and forgiveness.

PRAY

Lord Jesus, may my faith in you never waver. May it inspire me to imitate your healing ministry in every way my gifts and talents allow. Amen.

Saturday, December 5
First Saturday of Advent

BEGIN

Let your heart prepare him room.

PRAY

> He will give you rain for the seed that you sow in the ground, and the wheat that the soil produces will be rich and abundant.
>
> ~*Isaiah 30:23a*

LISTEN

Read Matthew 9:35–10:1, 5a, 6–8.

> Then Jesus said to his disciples, "The harvest is abundant but the laborers are few; so ask the master of the harvest to send out laborers for his harvest."
>
> ~*Matthew 9:37–38*

Give the Gift You Have Received

While I was a trustee at a local museum, signage came up at a board meeting. As the group was discussing the content of the prospective sign, I told them that when they had made up their minds, a friend of mine could create the sign at no cost to the museum. One trustee looked at me incredulously and asked, "And why would he do that?" I answered, "That's the kind of friends I have; what kind do you have?"

All right, I'm not proud of the sarcasm, but I was telling the truth. I didn't have to ask the friend I had in mind, because I knew him well enough to know that, although he wasn't a commercial artist, he had the skills necessary to do the work and that he would be disappointed if he learned that he hadn't been asked.

He had a gift, and he shared it freely.

That's what we are called to do with the gift we have been given—faith in Jesus Christ. Jesus was talking to us as well as to his apostles when he said, as we read in today's gospel passage, "without cost you have received; without cost you are to give."

We either grew up in that faith or acquired it as adults. In this passage, we hear Jesus calling us to be evangelists by letting others know about our faith, by sharing it with them directly, without embarrassment, and by demonstrating it in how we perform even the most ordinary tasks of daily life.

Advent is a perfect opportunity to carry out this mission. How we speak about our anticipation of the Christmas celebration and how we prepare ourselves and our homes can let others know that Christ is at the center of our lives and is eager to be at the center of theirs.

ACT

Today, I will be open to opportunities to share with others my faith in Jesus Christ as the Savior of the world.

PRAY

Lord Jesus, you called on your disciples to spread the Good News that you are the Savior of the world. May the Holy Spirit inspire and fortify me so that I may respond to that call without embarrassment but with gentleness and persistence. Amen.

Sunday, December 6
Second Week of Advent

BEGIN

Let your heart prepare him room.

PRAY

> The rugged land shall be made a plain, the rough
> country, a broad valley. Then the glory of the LORD
> shall be revealed, and all people shall see it together.
>
> ~*Isaiah 40:4–5*

LISTEN

Read Mark 1:1–8.

> John the Baptist appeared in the desert, proclaiming a
> baptism of repentance for the forgiveness of sins.
>
> ~*Mark 1:4*

Straighten the Path

A little more than a year ago, we saw and heard ads
promoting the movie *Downton Abbey*. The movie found
the household of an English manor in a tizzy because
King George V and Queen Mary had invited themselves
for an overnight stay. The reaction among the family
upstairs and the servants "below stairs" was true to
life, in a way. In countries that have monarchies, there
is frequently a lot of frenetic preparation wherever the
king, queen, or both are planning to travel. This spirit of
preparation is reflected in the gospel passage for today's
Mass. Mark writes about the mission of John the Baptist
by quoting the prophecy of Isaiah: "A voice of one crying

out in the desert: 'Prepare the way of the Lord, make straight his paths.'"

This prophecy is also cited in the gospels of Matthew, Luke, and John. In fact, the author of John's gospel puts the words in the Baptist's own mouth. The prophet's reference to a straight path implies that a path is now crooked in a way that is an obstacle to the Lord. Given the context, the evangelists seem to be telling us that something may be preventing the Lord from reaching us, and what could that something be if not a factor in our own lives?

Straightening out the path means straightening out ourselves. That can mean repenting and making amends for a serious sin, but more often it can mean eliminating some habit, inclination, or attitude that keeps us from recognizing God as the center of our lives. Straightening the path could mean weighing every decision we make and action we take, no matter how mundane, by what would please God and—by doing so—opening ourselves to a deeper and more intimate relationship with our Creator.

ACT

I will spend some time thinking today about activities or distractions that stand in the way of a fully loving relationship with God, and I will include those parts of my life in a sincere Act of Contrition.

PRAY

Creator God, the goal of my earthly life is to spend my eternal life in your presence. May I be aware of any practice, tendency, or desire with which I impede my own path to that goal. May I reform my life in order to please you and live with you forever. Amen.

Monday, December 7
Second Week of Advent

BEGIN

Let your heart prepare him room.

PRAY

> Say to those whose hearts are frightened: Be strong,
> fear not! Here is your God, he comes with vindica-
> tion; With divine recompense he comes to save you.
>
> *~Isaiah 35:4*

LISTEN

Read Luke 5:17–26.

> Jesus knew their thoughts and said to them in reply,
> "What are you thinking in your hearts? Which is eas-
> ier, to say, 'Your sins are forgiven,' or to say, 'Rise and
> walk'? But that you may know that the Son of Man
> has authority on earth to forgive sins"—he said to the
> one who was paralyzed, "I say to you, rise, pick up
> your stretcher, and go home."
>
> *~Luke 5:22–24*

Take Up the Cross

Aurelius Ambrosius, whom we know today as St.
Ambrose, did an excellent job as bishop of Milan, especially for someone who did not want the job.

Ambrose, whose memorial we observe today, was
governor of the city of Milan in the fourth century. The
bishop of Milan at the time had adopted the Arian heresy
that rejected the doctrine of the Trinity. When that bishop
died, the struggle between Arians and orthodox Christians erupted in violence. When Ambrose intervened in

an attempt to restore peace, there was a popular movement to make him bishop.

Ambrose, age thirty-three, had not yet received any sacraments and had not studied theology, and the fighting he had witnessed must have impressed on him what a difficult role a bishop played. So, he went into hiding.

After pressure from the Roman Emperor Gratian, however, Ambrose gave in. He was baptized, ordained a priest, and consecrated a bishop. As bishop, Ambrose actively helped the poor, opposed heresies, courageously worked to avoid violence, and assisted those who were jeopardized by the constant warfare in Europe.

None of us are likely to be called to a role as difficult and dangerous as the role Ambrose filled. But we are all called by baptism to participate in the ministry of Jesus. We are called to intentional acts of charity, mercy, forgiveness, and justice. Perhaps we do not go into hiding, as Ambrose initially did, in order to avoid these ministries, but if we avoid ministry by making excuses or by simply ignoring the Gospel, it amounts to the same thing.

As we anticipate the birth of Jesus during Advent, let us recall that the child we will adore in the manger grew to be the priest, prophet, and king who challenged us to carry on his work on earth.

ACT

I will remember as I go about my routine tasks today that whenever I touch the lives of others—strangers, friends, or family—I do it in the name of our Lord and Savior.

PRAY

Creator God, Advent is a season of new beginnings. May it be a new beginning of my dedication to the commission I received in Baptism to make your loving care present in the world through the generous acts I do in the name of your Son, Jesus Christ. Amen.

TUESDAY, DECEMBER 8

SOLEMNITY OF THE IMMACULATE CONCEPTION

BEGIN

Let your heart prepare him room.

PRAY

> God chose us in him, before the foundation of the
> world, to be holy and without blemish before him. In
> love he destined us for adoption to himself through
> Jesus Christ.
>
> ~Ephesians 1:4–5

LISTEN

Read Luke 1:26–38.

> The Holy Spirit will come upon you, and the power
> of the Most High will overshadow you. Therefore the
> child to be born will be called holy, the Son of God.
>
> ~Luke 1:35

Imitate Mary, Our Mother

The story of Adam and Eve conveys fundamental truths:
God created human nature out of nothing and gave
human beings understanding, a free will, and a spirit
that lives forever—and human beings have sinned by
doing what they knew was contrary to God's will. Every
sin consists of a person deliberately exercising his or her
free will contrary to God's will.

The Church teaches that human beings were created in innocence and that every human being has been
affected by the first sin committed. The effect is called

"original sin." We are cleansed of original sin at Baptism, but we remain free to exercise our will either in tune with or contrary to God's will. Jesus, conceived by the Holy Spirit, was not touched by original sin; and Mary, his mother, was conceived in her mother's womb without the mark of original sin—that's the Immaculate Conception. Mary still had a free will, and she exercised it in the incident described in Luke's gospel. The angel told her that in her unmarried and virginal state, she would bear a son, and how did she answer?

"I am the handmaid of the Lord. May it be done to me according to your word." In other words, not *my* will, but God's will, be done. The Church teaches that throughout her life, Mary exercised her free will in keeping with the will of God—that she never sinned. Mary is the model of the kind of life every one of us can strive for. Even if we falter, we can begin again by fixing our attention on her, acknowledging how we have fallen short of her example, and saying with her in prayer to God our Father: "your will be done on earth as it is in heaven."

ACT

I will spend a few minutes today thinking about the times when I have said "no" to God's will; pray for a part in God's inexhaustible mercy; and resolve that, when I am aware of God's call to me, I will say with Mary, "Your will be done."

PRAY

Mary, mother of our Savior, I am inspired by your eager submission to God's will. I pray that you will accompany me whenever I fail to imitate your faithfulness but resolve to reconcile with God. Amen.

Wednesday, December 9
Second Week of Advent

BEGIN

Let your heart prepare him room.

PRAY

> They that hope in the LORD will renew their strength,
> they will soar as with eagles' wings.
>
> ~Isaiah 40:31a

LISTEN

Read Matthew 11:28–30.

> Jesus said to the crowds: "Come to me, all you who
> labor and are burdened, and I will give you rest."
>
> ~Matthew 11:28

He Walks beside You

Chances are Jesus knew something about yokes.

The Gospel of Mark implies that Jesus was a carpenter. If he had been, he might have made yokes, which were fashioned from wood. The yoke joins two oxen or other animals at their shoulders, so that they can evenly share a burden. Whether he made a yoke or watched his father make one, Jesus found the device to be an apt metaphor for the bond he offers to share with us. In his reference to the yoke in a passage in the Gospel of Matthew, Jesus says, "Take my yoke upon you and learn from me, for I am meek and humble of heart."

A yoke is usually made for two. If you were to accept that invitation, who would be the other party in the yoke? The answer is Jesus.

This metaphor emphasizes that Jesus came into the world to share the burden of our human nature in every way, except in sin. He knows that when he asks us to live lives of charity, justice, and mercy, he asks something that we are capable of doing with his assistance.

The yokes of Jesus' time were hand-carved and often fitted to specific animals. And the yoke that Jesus offers each of us is fashioned to suit our individual talents and resources. He doesn't ask all of us to take on the kind of mindless drudgery we associate with beasts of burden; rather he asks each of us to continue his own ministry in a way that flows naturally from our abilities and our state of life.

He promises that he will be alongside us every step of the way if we say yes to his invitation, have faith in his support, and commit ourselves to the work that he began.

ACT

I will try to be aware, today and every day, that Jesus is always beside me. I will make decisions with his presence in mind, and I will rely on his help in all things.

PRAY

Lord Jesus, please accompany me throughout my days. May the world always see in me someone fit to be your companion. Amen.

Thursday, December 10
Second Week of Advent

BEGIN

Let your heart prepare him room.

PRAY

> Your Kingdom is a Kingdom for all ages, and your
> dominion endures through all generations.
>
> *~Psalm 145:13*

LISTEN

Read Matthew 11:11–15.

> And if you are willing to accept it, he is Elijah, the
> one who is to come.
>
> *~Matthew 11:14*

The Kingdom Is at Hand

A literary device Jesus liked to use in his teaching was the paradox—a logical statement that seems to contradict itself. In the gospel reading for today's Mass, for example, Jesus says, "There has been none greater than John the Baptist; yet the least in the Kingdom of heaven is greater than he."

How can both statements be true? The greatness of John the Baptist was evident first in his role as the prophet who pointed not to himself but to Jesus as Savior of the world. John was also effective in calling people to repent their sins, and he fearlessly challenged the hypocrisy of the civil and religious leaders in first-century Israel.

But when Jesus made his remarks, John was in prison, and he would not emerge alive. The Christian view is that with John's death, the last of the great Jewish prophets passed. His death put the exclamation point, as it were, on the prophecy of Elijah that, nine hundred years before, had foretold the coming of the Messiah. Jesus' disciples would not relate to God through the old Law of Judaism but through the Son of God, enjoying an intimacy with God that had not been possible since the event we remember as the fall of Adam.

Jesus wasn't demeaning John's ministry nor questioning John's sanctity, and he was not suggesting that John would not rise to eternal life. Rather, Jesus was emphasizing the kingdom that was opening for those who followed him. It's impossible to miss the urgency of his message, as he concludes with "whoever has ears ought to hear." Advent is a good time for us to stop and listen, to reflect on how we are living in the kingdom that is not only in the future but, as John proclaimed, "is at hand."

ACT

Today, I will help the people around me recognize God's kingdom on earth by considering how I can be an instrument of his love in all my encounters.

PRAY

Almighty God, as I await the celebration of the birth of our Savior, may I live each moment as someone who knows that your kingdom is not in the future but is "at hand." May everything I do or say that affects another living thing, or the earth itself, reflect the grace of that kingdom. Amen.

FRIDAY, DECEMBER 11
SECOND WEEK OF ADVENT

BEGIN

Let your heart prepare him room.

PRAY

> I, the LORD, your God, teach you what is for your
> good, and lead you on the way you should go.
>
> *~Isaiah 48:17b*

LISTEN

Read Matthew 11:16–19.

> Wisdom is vindicated by her works.
>
> *~Matthew 11:19b*

Focus on What Matters

Jesus' remark in the gospel reading for today's Mass is
almost comical, as he tells the crowd, "For John came
neither eating nor drinking, and they said, 'He is pos-
sessed by a demon.' The Son of Man came eating and
drinking and they said, 'Look, he is a glutton and a
drunkard, a friend of tax collectors and sinners.'"

The way that Jesus framed this statement made the
critics appear ridiculous, highlighting their self-contra-
diction. Jesus' retort also should have made some folks
understand that whether or not John the Baptist or Jesus
ate or drank was irrelevant and that therefore it was
absurd to dwell on such matters. Those critics are no
different from people in our time who avoid confronting
the challenges of the Gospel by dwelling on matters not
central to our faith.

We have to expect that in a Church as diverse as ours there are going to be people of different philosophical strains; people with different tastes in liturgical practice; and people with different levels of engagement. But, whether or not he ate and drank, John taught that each of us should examine our lives and make any changes necessary to conform to the will of God. Whether or not he ate and drank, Jesus taught that each of us is called to reciprocate the unconditional love God offers us by loving God and our neighbor—our neighbor being anyone outside of ourselves.

We may think individual clerics or the whole Church is too liberal or too conservative; we may think that our own parish or the Church at large is too modern or too traditional. Perhaps over time we can sort those things out in dialogue with clergy and laity. But those issues should not distract us from self-evaluation, penance, reform, and lives defined by charity, mercy, and justice.

ACT

I will spend time today reaffirming my faith in the teachings of the Church as found in the Nicene Creed and on the real presence of Christ in his word, in the liturgical assembly, and in the sacraments.

PRAY

Come, Holy Spirit, and confirm my faith in the teaching of Jesus and of his Church. Help me to be patient and openhearted so that I may be a source of unity and not division in the Church. Amen.

SATURDAY, DECEMBER 12
FEAST OF OUR LADY OF GUADALUPE

BEGIN

Let your heart prepare him room.

PRAY

> Blessed are you, holy Virgin Mary, deserving of all praise;
> from you rose the sun of justice, Christ our God.
>
> ~*Gospel Acclamation*

LISTEN

Read Luke 1:26–38.

> Mary said, "Behold, I am the handmaid of the Lord.
> May it be done to me according to your word."
>
> ~*Luke 1:38a*

Mary Calls the Nations

When I was an altar server in the 1950s, one of my weekly duties was to assist at devotions to Our Lady of Fatima. Outside the church where my wife and I were married is a shrine to Our Lady of the Highway. In the city where my wife and I often vacation, we attend Mass at a church dedicated to Our Lady, Star of the Sea. Our current parish is Our Lady of Lourdes and, in another city, less than an hour's drive from our house, we attend a food festival at the church of Our Lady of Lebanon. About a year ago, my diocese was consecrated to Our Lady of Guadalupe.

In a way, attaching these titles to Mary, the mother of Jesus, may seem like a way of fragmenting devotion to her by associating her with particular places. But I prefer to think of it in exactly the opposite way. The multiplicity of titles that associate Mary with places such as Aparecida, Brazil; Knock, Ireland; Mount Carmel, Israel; and Cerro del Cabezo, Spain, reflect the universal character of her role as our spiritual mother.

The prophecy of Zechariah read in today's Mass tells the "daughter Zion" to sing and rejoice, because "many nations shall join themselves to the LORD . . . and they shall be his people." More than five hundred years later, Mary, a daughter of Zion and the representative of God's chosen people, accepted God's will that she play a critical role in fulfilling that prophecy. That role did not end with the events we read about in Advent and at Christmas; far beyond her place as the mother of Jesus, even beyond her place as his first disciple, Mary continues her mission as the "new Eve," the mother of every nation, calling all people to embrace the Christ and his Gospel.

ACT

Today, I will pray the Rosary, meditating on the Virgin Mary's example of obedience to God's will.

PRAY

Hail, Mary, full of grace. The Lord is with you. Blessed are you among women, and blessed is the fruit of your womb, Jesus. Holy Mary, Mother of God, pray for us sinners, now and at the hour of our death. Amen.

SUNDAY, DECEMBER 13
THIRD WEEK OF ADVENT

BEGIN

Let your heart prepare him room.

PRAY

> I rejoice heartily in the LORD, in my God is the joy of
> my soul.
>
> ~*Isaiah 61:10a*

LISTEN

Read 1 Thessalonian 5:16–24.

> Rejoice always. Pray without ceasing. In all circum-
> stances give thanks, for this is the will of God for you
> in Christ Jesus.
>
> ~*1 Thessalonians 5:16–18*

He Lights Our Way

We all have heard the saying "It was so dark that I
couldn't see my hand in front of my face." Yet we rarely
experience darkness that profound. If there is even the
smallest source of light, our eyes will adjust until we can
see some of our surroundings.

But it is possible to experience total darkness. For
example, Jewel Cave in Custer, South Dakota, offers this
opportunity. As visitors climb down more than seven
hundred steps in this third-longest cave in the world,
the procession pauses and the lights go out, and there
is total darkness. If you have experienced anything like
that, you may have felt uneasy as the seconds ticked
away and your eyes did not perform the adjustment that

you usually take for granted. You may have experienced some joy when light was restored.

Why reflect on this experience today? Because this is Gaudete Sunday, when we are prompted to rejoice, as we read today in the prophecy of Isaiah. The cause of our rejoicing is the light that "shines in the darkness," as the Gospel of John proclaims, and as John the Baptist, who "was not himself the light," loudly testified.

We rejoice because ours is not a faith of hopelessness but a faith of hope. If we have faith in the Savior whose birth we soon will celebrate, we never need to feel the dread imposed by total darkness. Jesus offers forgiveness and reconciliation to anyone who turns to him for healing. What's more, he calls on those who love him to be the light of charity and comfort for each other. No matter how far we descend into the cave, he is our light; and we in turn, as he reminds us in Matthew's gospel, are to be "the light of the world."

ACT

Amid the colors and sounds of today, I will try to intentionally recall, and thank God, that the reason for our joy is the coming of our Savior.

PRAY

Jesus Christ, our Savior, may I find true joy in this season by welcoming you again into my heart and by dedicating myself again to reflecting your love wherever I go. Amen.

MONDAY, DECEMBER 14
THIRD WEEK OF ADVENT

BEGIN

Let your heart prepare him room.

PRAY

> Your ways, O LORD, make known to me; teach me
> your paths.
>
> *~Psalm 25:4*

LISTEN

> *Read Matthew 21:23–27.*
>
> Jesus himself said to them, "Neither shall I tell you by
> what authority I do these things."
>
> *~Matthew 21:27*

Be Still and Know that I Am God

As an undergraduate student, I worked at the university
radio station and learned about "dead air"—any lapse of
time in which there was no music, no voice, only silence.

I learned that while ten seconds of silence is not
noticeable in everyday life, it seems like an eternity
during a radio broadcast. Today, on the other hand, we
observe the memorial of St. John of the Cross, a man of
the sixteenth century who spent his life seeking silence.

John was attracted to the contemplative life in orders
such as the Carthusians, but under the influence of St.
Teresa of Ávila, he introduced reforms—including more
silence—within his own order, the Carmelites. These
reforms caused a rift among the Carmelites and tensions
rose so high that John was imprisoned by members of

his order and subjected to physical punishment. But he escaped and the dispute among the Carmelites was eventually resolved, and John went about his work.

"What we need most in order to make progress," John wrote, "is to be silent before this great God with our appetite and with our tongue, for the language he best hears is silent love."

While most of us don't yearn for the silence of a hermitage, we all should try to regularly be alone with God. This is a prescription for a healthy spiritual life at any time, but Advent, which points us toward the appearance of Immanuel, "God with us," is the perfect season to jumpstart the habit, to shut out of our minds, each day for ten or fifteen minutes, the distractions that occupy the place that belongs to him. We can know intellectually that God is always present, but silent contemplation, a time of intimacy with the One who loves us, can help us know this in our souls.

ACT

I will seriously consider how I can find ten minutes out of today to spend in silent companionship with God.

PRAY

Creator God, you know my thoughts and you know what I need, so you do not need my words. May I be silent before you, comforted by your presence and guided by your will. Amen.

TUESDAY, DECEMBER 15
THIRD WEEK OF ADVENT

BEGIN

Let your heart prepare him room.

PRAY

> I will change and purify the lips of the peoples, that they may call upon the name of the Lord, to serve him with one accord.
>
> ~*Zephaniah 3:9*

LISTEN

> *Read Psalm 34:2–3, 6–7, 17–18, 19 and 23.*
>
> The Lord redeems the lives of his servants; no one incurs guilt who takes refuge in him.
>
> ~*Psalm 34:23*

Better Late than Never

When I was growing up, my family operated a grocery store where I accumulated many fond memories. I have also retained one uncomfortable memory involving a sign that my father had hung in the store: "Closed on Sunday. See you in church."

I knew most customers by name, and one day a stranger arrived, but the conversation between my father and this man revealed that they had known each other sometime in the past.

The man pointed at the sign and asked my father, "Is this true?" When my father nodded yes, the man said, "Wow. Things must have changed!"

My father, who knew that I was listening, blushed at that remark and didn't respond. At the time, my father never missed Sunday Mass and was the chief usher at our church. I don't think Dad was ever the playboy of the Western world, but the implication of our visitor's remark, and his tone of voice, was that Dad was a worldly figure in his early days.

Whatever that meant in real terms, it did change, as our sarcastic caller remarked. This kind of transformation is what Jesus was talking about in the gospel passage for today's Mass. When Jesus talked to the chief priests and elders about conversion, he used the extreme examples of tax collectors and prostitutes, but clearly there were many more ordinary people such as my father who turned from indifference and self-indulgence to worship and service.

During Advent when—even amid the clamor and excess—awareness of the coming of the Savior is heightened, we can pray that those who have not yet been touched by the Gospel of penance and forgiveness will at last turn to the Lord who rejoices in latecomers.

ACT

I will pray today for those whose faith has been shaken, for those whose faith is weak, and for those who profess no faith.

PRAY

O Jesus, you who rejoice in finding what was lost, may Advent be the occasion for many to find refuge in you and fellowship in the assembly of your disciples. Amen.

WEDNESDAY, DECEMBER 16
THIRD WEEK OF ADVENT

BEGIN

Let your heart prepare him room.

PRAY

> Turn to me and be safe, all you ends of the earth, for I
> am God; there is no other!

> ~Isaiah 45:22

LISTEN

Read Luke 7:18b–23.

> The blind regain their sight, the lame walk, lepers are
> cleansed, the deaf hear, the dead are raised, the poor
> have the good news proclaimed to them.

> ~Luke 7:22

Don't Look for Another

We have patron saints of bell makers, wool combers,
surfers, and chimney sweeps and, if we wanted to, we
could have a patron saint of doubters. The title could go
to the apostle Thomas, but today's gospel passage raises
another candidate: John the Baptist.

John, imprisoned by Herod Antipas and probably
realizing that death is near, sends a delegation to ask
Jesus, "Are you 'He who is to come,' or do we look for
someone else?" This is the same John who once direct-
ed his own disciples' attention to Jesus and declared,
"Behold, the Lamb of God."

John's doubt probably was born of impatience. A
firebrand, he wanted to see hypocrites such as Herod

called to account, and perhaps Jesus wasn't enough of a revolutionary for him. We could find this doubt scandalous—if most of us, whether or not we acknowledge it, did not experience doubt at some point in our lives. "Most of us" includes not only John and Thomas Didymus but also the likes of St. Teresa of Calcutta, St. Thérèse of Lisieux, and Thomas Merton. We're in good company when we doubt.

While we may be reluctant to concede our doubt, no less an authority than Pope Benedict XVI has said that, if anything, we should expect it, that vacillating between believing and not believing is part of the "dilemma" of being human. When we deal with our Catholic faith, we deal with mystery, and in mystery certainty eludes us. A few verses after today's gospel passage, however, Luke writes that Jesus said, "I assure you, there is no man born of woman greater than John." Although his belief was momentarily shaken, John persisted. In doing so, he was a model for us, the patron of both our doubt and our ultimate faith in the Son of God.

ACT

If my faith is shaken by doubt today, I will pray for God's reassurance and share my doubts with a pastor, confessor, or spiritual director.

PRAY

Holy Spirit, Source of Wisdom, be with me when I am in doubt. Give me persistence and clarity of vision so that I may seek the truth and finally rest in your consolation. Amen.

Thursday, December 17
Third Week of Advent

BEGIN

Let your heart prepare him room.

PRAY

> In him shall all the tribes of the earth be blessed; all
> the nations shall proclaim his happiness.

> ~Psalm 72:17

LISTEN

Read Matthew 1:1–17.

> Jacob [became] the father of Joseph, the husband of
> Mary. Of her was born Jesus who is called the Christ.

> ~Matthew 1:16

We Are His Disciples

Domenico De Rosa and Geronima Torino were my
great-great-great-great-great grandparents, and their
names are among the information I have accumulated
while researching the genealogy of my family. Much of
the information is more detailed, such as the fact that a
second cousin was appointed the official White House
pianist by President John F. Kennedy.

The genealogy in today's gospel reading perhaps
cannot be taken as literally as mine or yours. It is the
genealogy of Joseph, who was not the biological father
of Jesus. The author of the gospel was not interested
in constructing a family tree, as I have been doing, but
rather in establishing a foundation for the identity and
ministry of Jesus. By calling Jesus "Christ" and then "son

of David, son of Abraham," the writer was establishing from the beginning that Jesus was the long-awaited Messiah, the fulfillment of promises God had made to the Jewish people over the ages.

In addition, some scholars say, by including the names of women—which was not a Jewish practice at the time—along with Gentiles in the genealogy, the author was anticipating that Jesus' ministry would extend beyond the traditions and boundaries of Israel. By including people known to be serious sinners, the writer was reflecting on the unlimited mercy of God—a critical theme in Jesus' teaching. As a whole, the genealogy points to Jesus as the one to offer a new trajectory for humanity, as he encouraged people to move beyond their comfort zones of ethnic group or social circle and embrace a new relationship with others in Christ.

Clearly, this transformation is not complete in our own time. Continuing to spread Jesus' message of love, and practicing it in our own lives, is our duty as disciples of the "son of David, son of Abraham."

ACT

Today, I will play my part in Jesus' inclusive ministry by treating everyone I meet with a generous heart and open mind.

PRAY

Jesus, my Savior, you fulfilled the promise made to Israel and invited the whole world to a new age of peace and justice. May I always play my part in that new age by imitating your charity and compassion. Amen.

Friday, December 18
Third Week of Advent

BEGIN

Let your heart prepare him room.

PRAY

> For he shall rescue the poor when he cries out, and
> the afflicted when he has no one to help him.
>
> *~Psalm 72:12*

LISTEN

Read Matthew 1:18-25.

> When Joseph awoke, he did as the angel of the Lord
> had commanded him and took his wife into his
> home.
>
> *~Matthew 1:24*

Care for Those in Your Charge

We once took our children on a family weekend at a
retreat house. Among the families present there was a
youngish couple who had three little children of their
own—enough to keep parents very busy—and two
mentally challenged adult men whom the couple had
formally adopted. Parenthood is one of the biggest com-
mitments of a lifetime, but this young couple made a
choice to carry their commitment beyond its already
weighty implications.

That can be said, too, of Joseph. The gospel tells us
that Joseph was "a righteous man" who wanted to min-
imize the trouble Mary would experience because of
her pregnancy. But Joseph was urged through a divine

revelation to take responsibility not only for Mary but also for a son who would "save his people from their sins." Many of us have heard this story, particularly during Advent, all of our lives. It's hard to imagine the reaction of a man hearing this command for the first time.

But if Joseph questioned the divine message or hesitated to accept the role that he was offered, the author of the gospel does not say so. Instead, the writer says simply that "when Joseph awoke, he did as the angel of the Lord had commanded him." Joseph's calm acceptance of responsibility is a model for all who raise children in more conventional circumstances. It is a model for we who in any way have the well-being of others in our charge: students, employees, infirm parents, even strangers who, Jesus says, are our neighbors. Just as Joseph gave up what may have been a placid single life in order to care for Mary and her child, we too are called to give up some comfort to nurture the lives of others.

ACT

When it is within my power to help, support, or comfort another person today, I will not be deterred by the inconvenience to me.

PRAY

St. Joseph, guardian of Jesus and Mary, may I always be as unselfish as you when I know that I have the means of helping others, not only in my family but wherever life takes me. Amen.

SATURDAY, DECEMBER 19
THIRD WEEK OF ADVENT

BEGIN

Let your heart prepare him room.

PRAY

> O God, you have taught me from my youth, and till
> the present I proclaim your wondrous deeds.
>
> *~Psalm 71:17*

LISTEN

Read Luke 1:5–25.

> I was sent to speak to you and to announce to you
> this good news. But now you will be speechless and
> unable to talk . . . because you did not believe my
> words.
>
> *~Luke 1:19b–20*

Hear the Word of the Lord

When they were young, my children and I used to play
"Who can go the longest without talking?" If each of
them had gone off alone, the silence might have lasted
a while, but as we sat around the kitchen table staring at
each other, it was usually only a matter of minutes before
one of them blurted out some remark.

   That wasn't surprising. Speech seems to come more
naturally to human beings than silence. Sometimes, we
seem more interested in hearing ourselves talk than in
listening to someone else. Perhaps the archangel Gabriel,
in today's gospel passage, was teaching Zechariah a lesson about that human tendency to talk rather than listen.

Admittedly, Gabriel's message was astounding, but notice that Zechariah didn't respond to what the angel had said about the child who would be John the Baptist: "He will be great in the sight of the Lord," "filled with the Holy Spirit," and destined to "prepare a people fit for the Lord." No, Zechariah, as though he hadn't heard those extravagant predictions, objected only that he and his wife, Elizabeth, were too old to bear children.

I don't accept the usual explanation that what happened next was Gabriel's way of punishing Zechariah for arguing. Rather, I think Gabriel deprived Zechariah of speech so the father-to-be would have time to contemplate what God had done—on God's terms, not on his own. It's a good lesson for us, too, particularly in this season. We have almost a week before we will celebrate the birth of the Savior of the world, the Savior of each one of us. As hectic as this week may be, let's set aside time each day to be still and silent, to focus on the child Jesus and the man he became, and listen to what God speaks directly to our hearts.

ACT

Today, I will pause to meditate on the mystery that God loved us so much that he embraced human nature by taking on the form of a newborn child.

PRAY

Almighty God, may I always try to discern your will for me and never let the noise of everyday life drown out your voice. Amen.

SUNDAY, DECEMBER 20
FOURTH WEEK OF ADVENT

BEGIN

Let your heart prepare him room.

PRAY

> The favors of the LORD I will sing forever; through
> all generations my mouth shall proclaim your
> faithfulness.

> ~*Psalm 89:2*

LISTEN

> *Read Luke 1:26–38.*

> Mary said, "Behold, I am the handmaid of the Lord.
> May it be done to me according to your word."

> ~*Luke 1:38*

God Called Mary, and He Calls Us

One of the best retellings of the Gospel was *Jesus of Nazareth*, the 1977 television miniseries. The director, Franco Zeffirelli, presented the life of Jesus in a realistic environment that viewers could accept as first-century Palestine. This realism was on display in scenes of everyday life and in the supernatural elements of the story: the miracles of Jesus and, of special relevance to today's gospel passage, the annunciation to Mary.

There is no winged angel in this scene. Mary is asleep in her unadorned room but wakes to see an intense light streaming through the opening that serves as a window. The viewer hears no angelic voice, but the terrified Mary responds to a message that penetrates her heart: "How can that be? No man has ever touched me." She slowly kneels on the ground and responds, "Behold the handmaiden of the Lord."

No other human being will experience exactly what Mary experienced, but every human being does share in this: God speaks to our hearts and makes his will known to us. We don't see angels, we don't hear voices, but we know what God asks of us. What God asks isn't as dramatic as what he asked of Mary, but it isn't child's play either. God asks that we live as disciples of Mary's son by putting the general welfare, the well-being of individual people, and the health of the planet we live on ahead of our own comfort and convenience

This may not be our first instinct, conditioned as we are to pursue self-preservation, but it is what God asks—lives in which every choice is governed by charity, mercy, and justice. God asked a lot of Mary, and she said yes. As our celebration of the birth of her son approaches, let us pause each day to ask if we, too, are saying yes.

ACT

I will prayerfully read the account of the Annunciation to Mary in the Gospel of Luke and meditate on Mary's faithfulness in putting aside her doubts and questions and accepting God's will.

PRAY

Holy Mary, mother of Jesus, may my contemplation of your decision to accept God's will for you inspire me to always put divine wisdom before my own desires. Amen.

MONDAY, DECEMBER 21
FOURTH WEEK OF ADVENT

BEGIN

Let your heart prepare him room.

PRAY

> Shout for joy, O daughter Zion! Sing joyfully, O Israel!
> Be glad and exult with all your heart, O daughter
> Jerusalem!
>
> ~*Zephaniah 3:14*

LISTEN

Read Luke 1:39–45.

> Blessed are you who believed that what was spoken
> to you by the Lord would be fulfilled.
>
> ~*Luke 1:45*

The Spirit Is upon You

Scripture is peppered with men and women who appear
in a critical scene or two and then vanish. Nicodemus,
Zacchaeus, and the Samaritan woman at Jacob's well
come to mind.

Another example is Elizabeth, described in most
translations of the Bible as a "kinswoman" or "relative"
of the Virgin Mary. All we know of Elizabeth is that,
according to Luke's gospel, she was childless, sterile, and
"advanced in years"; a descendent of Moses' brother,
Aaron; and, with her husband, Zechariah, "righteous in
the eyes of God, observing all the commandments and
ordinances of the Lord blamelessly." We also know that,
as an angel had promised Zechariah and Mary, Elizabeth

bore a son whom we know as John the Baptist. We never hear of her again. But Elizabeth is not an incidental character in the gospel, and not only because she was "righteous" and "blameless" before giving birth to John.

We cannot overlook the author's comment, in today's gospel passage, that Elizabeth was "filled with the Holy Spirit" as she exuberantly welcomed Mary. This encounter occurred before the foundation of the Church, when the Holy Spirit descended on the apostles and fortified them to spread the Gospel, and before the institution of the sacrament in which the Holy Spirit confirms us in the faith and commissions us, too, to carry on the ministry of Jesus.

We cannot know how much Elizabeth knew about what was happening through her and through Mary, but the gospel makes it clear that Elizabeth understood her role to be the will of God and not only accepted this but was overjoyed by it. In the Sacrament of Confirmation, we are filled with the same Holy Spirit that enlivened Elizabeth. Her appearance in our Advent reflections is an opportunity to reflect on how exuberantly, how joyfully, we can accept the role God has given us.

ACT

I will let my joy at being a disciple of Jesus warm the hearts of everyone I encounter today.

PRAY

I am grateful, Lord Jesus, that you have called me to be your disciple. I gladly accept that role, and I will spread your Gospel with joy. Amen.

TUESDAY, DECEMBER 22
FOURTH WEEK OF ADVENT

BEGIN

Let your heart prepare him room.

PRAY

> He raises the needy from the dust; from the dung
> heap he lifts up the poor, to seat them with nobles.
>
> *~1 Samuel 2:8*

LISTEN

> *Read Luke 1:46–56.*
>
> My soul proclaims the greatness of the Lord; my spir-
> it rejoices in God my savior.
>
> *~Luke 1:46–47*

Help God Lift Up the Lowly

My favorite moment in the Liturgy of the Hours comes
during Evening Prayer when we recite the Magnificat,
which makes up most of today's gospel passage. As we
read these verses, we can sense that they poured out
of Mary after she was greeted by Elizabeth. To those
who savor this poem or song, it may be jarring to read a
widely circulated story claiming that the World War II–
era Archbishop of Canterbury, William Temple, advised
Anglican missionaries in India not to read the Magnificat
in public.

His rationale ostensibly was that, because of the
abject poverty and social inequality in India, some listen-
ers might hear revolution brewing in Mary's words—her
praise of a God who casts down the mighty from their

thrones and fills the hungry with good things while he sends the rich away empty. I have seen many people, including preachers, repeat this story about Archbishop Temple, who was in fact a champion of the working class, but I have never verified that the story is true. In any event, it's unlikely that Mary had revolution on her mind during her joyous visit with Elizabeth—at least, not the violent revolution one associates with mobs and armies. Rather, her poetry was more likely a prophecy concerning the ministry of the son she soon would bear.

Jesus' ministry was indeed revolutionary, but in the sense that it envisioned a world in which the strong cared for the weak, the prosperous lifted up the needy, and all persons made the well-being of others as important as their own. That's a revolution that is far from complete, and this season, as Charles Dickens wrote, "a time, of all others, when want is keenly felt and abundance rejoices," is a good time to consider what part we are playing. Do our actions this season perpetuate the inequality and injustice of the world, or do they contribute to a more just society?

ACT

I will meditate on what role God has for me in renewing the world and, like Mary, I will not shrink from it.

PRAY

O blessed Mary, may I imitate you in believing that I have the ability to play a part in building God's kingdom on earth, through your son, our Lord, Jesus Christ. Amen.

WEDNESDAY, DECEMBER 23
FOURTH WEEK OF ADVENT

BEGIN

Let your heart prepare him room.

PRAY

> And suddenly there will come to the temple the LORD
> whom you seek, and the messenger of the covenant
> whom you desire.
>
> ~*Malachi 3:1b*

LISTEN

Read Luke 1:57–66.

> He asked for a tablet and wrote, "John is his name."
> . . . All who heard these things took them to heart,
> saying, "What, then, will this child be? For surely the
> hand of the Lord was with him."
>
> ~*Luke 1:63b, 66*

A Time for Renewal

Two friends in my childhood were Jack and Jackie. Both
of them were baptized with the name of John, but so
were their fathers, so the families adopted nicknames
to avoid confusion when someone referred to "John."
The parents didn't give the boys the same name as their
fathers due to a lack of imagination. They did it because
of the tradition in many cultures in which children are
named after their forebears.

This tradition was common among the Jewish
people when John the Baptist was born. So, we read in
today's gospel passage that when Elizabeth said that

her son was to be named John, the busybodies objected that no one else in the family had that name. The name, which means "God is gracious," was dictated by the archangel Gabriel when he informed Zechariah that Elizabeth would bear a child. Beyond the implication that this child was the gift of a gracious God, Gabriel didn't give a reason for this breach of custom.

But whatever the divine purpose may have been, the choice of a name that departed from the norm was appropriate for this child, because, as a man, he would encourage people to break with their past, to reform—perhaps better expressed as re-form—their lives. "Let the man with two coats give to him who has none. The man who has food should do the same." Or, more bluntly, "Taxpayers, soldiers—anyone—don't take advantage of people just because you've been getting away with it until now." John's desert life, his rough appearance and primitive diet, along with these challenging ideas, would foreshadow the radical nature of the teaching of Jesus—something new under the sun. We can use these last hours of Advent to consider how our celebration of the birth of Jesus might inspire something new in our lives.

ACT

I will identify one aspect of my life that I can reform to move me closer to the ideals preached by John and Jesus.

PRAY

Lord Jesus Christ, may I never shrink from the challenges in the preaching of John the Baptist and in your teaching and example. I pray that the coming celebration of your birth will inspire in me a new and deeper commitment to live as your disciple. Amen.

THURSDAY, DECEMBER 24
FOURTH WEEK OF ADVENT

BEGIN

Let your heart prepare him room.

PRAY

> He shall say of me, "You are my father, my God, the rock, my savior." Forever I will maintain my kindness toward him, and my covenant with him stands firm.

> *~Psalm 89:27, 29*

LISTEN

Read Luke 1:67–79.

> [God sets us] free to worship him without fear, holy and righteous in his sight all the days of our life.

> *~Luke 1:74b–75*

Make Straight His Path

When the archangel Gabriel deprived Zechariah of the ability to speak, there was no mention of the ability to hear. But in yesterday's gospel passage we read that when folks asked Zechariah about his son's name, they did so by using signs. In other words, Zechariah had become not only mute but also deaf.

Once Zechariah answered by writing on a wax tablet, his ability to hear and speak was restored, and he immediately burst into the hymn we read in the passage for today's Mass. There are two parts to this song. In the first part, Zechariah thanks God for fulfilling the ancient promise to Israel of a deliverer, the Messiah, who would lead his people not to temporal but to spiritual freedom.

In the second part, Zechariah proclaims the mission of his son who "will go before the Lord to prepare his way, to give his people knowledge of salvation"—practically the same words John will use to explain his role with relation to the Messiah.

In our own way, we too are called to prepare straight paths for the Christ. The adage that we read on lawn signs and car magnets, "Keep Christ in Christmas," doesn't express half the challenge—keeping Christ in everyday life. As society is increasingly infected with self-absorption, greed, materialism, and incivility, who—if not we—will clear the way for the Lord?

At Christmastime, when our Christian identity is perhaps most evident, we can let others know that our celebration—whatever its exterior signs—is principally about the birth of the One who calls us to lives of love, mercy, and peace. And through the coming year, we can continue to make a path for the Lord, by sharing how our faith informs our daily lives and by gently inviting others to share our peace and our joy.

ACT

As I anticipate the celebration of the birth of our Savior, I will resolve to bring the optimism and joy of these last hours of Advent into the weeks and months of the new year, not for my own satisfaction but for the benefit of everyone I meet.

PRAY

Creator God, thank you for the gift I am about to celebrate, the birth of your Son in whom you have redeemed the world. May I always demonstrate my gratitude by living according to your will. Amen.

FRIDAY, DECEMBER 25
SOLEMNITY OF THE NATIVITY OF OUR LORD

BEGIN

Let your heart prepare him room.

PRAY

> For a child is born to us, a son is given us; upon his shoulder dominion rests.

> ~Isaiah 9:6a

LISTEN

Read Luke 2:1–14.

> For today in the city of David a savior has been born for you who is Christ and Lord.

> ~Luke 2:11

Let All Adore Him

When my children and their children were born, their first visitors were their grandparents. This seemed, to our family, to be a privilege to which grandparents had a natural right. Yet this wasn't the case when Jesus was born. His grandparents might have been in Nazareth, about ninety miles away, and they are not mentioned in the gospels. So far as we know, the first visitors Jesus received were shepherds who had learned of his birth through divine revelation.

Although they had to be both tough and highly skilled in order to nurture and protect large flocks of animals, shepherds were thought of as a low caste, unfit company for respectable people. We can see in the shepherds the outcasts that Jesus holds most dear. The shepherds were devoted to the sheep and goats in their care to the point of accounting for every one of them, no matter what that took, and risking their lives in warding off thieves and predatory animals—foreshadowing the devotion and sacrifice of the Good Shepherd.

Most important, before Jesus set out in search of the "lost sheep," people were attracted to him, came to him. It isn't enough to have heard of Christ in revelation and to have accepted him as the Son of God. Like the shepherds, we must go to him—in prayer, in the Eucharist, in the faces of so many who need care and attention—not only today but every day.

"O come, let us adore him!"

ACT

I will imitate the Holy Family throughout the year by being hospitable to people of good will without judging them on the basis of their appearance or social standing.

PRAY

Lord Jesus, today we celebrate the holy day on which the Virgin Mary gave birth to you. May I give birth to you every day by ministering in your name to those who are in material or spiritual need. Glory and praise to you who live and reign with the Father and the Holy Spirit, one God, forever and ever. Amen.

Charles Paolino is managing editor at RENEW International. He is a permanent deacon of the Diocese of Metuchen, New Jersey, ministering in liturgy, preaching, and adult education at Our Lady of Lourdes Church in Whitehouse Station. He also is a columnist for The Catholic Spirit, the newspaper and website of the Diocese of Metuchen, and a freelance theater critic. He is the author of four books in The Living Gospel series.

Paolino spent forty-three years in newspaper journalism and more than thirty years as an adjunct instructor of English at multiple universities and colleges, including Seton Hall and Rutgers. He earned a bachelor's degree in communications from Seton Hall and a master's degree in journalism from Penn State. He and his wife, Patricia Ann, live in Whitehouse Station. They have four children and six grandchildren.